His Royal Dogness,

Guy the Beagle

The Rebarkable True Story of Meghan Markle's Rescue Dog

BY

Guy the Beagle

WITH MICHAEL BRUMM AND CAMILLE MARCH

ILLUSTRATED BY EG KELLER

Simon & Schuster

NEW YORK   LONDON   TORONTO   SYDNEY   NEW DELHI

MICHAEL BRUMM AND CAMILLE MARCH:

FOR HENRY & BEA

EG KELLER:

FOR SCOUT

My story begins, like many, in the woods of Kentucky.

I was lost and living alone, surrounded by tulip trees,

myrtle bushes, and cranky squirrels.

But as luck would have it,
a nice person found me and
moved me to an animal shelter.

I soon learned that an animal shelter is a lot like a public restroom—
you want to spend as little time in one as possible.

Sadly, despite my best tail wags, no one in Kentucky came to adopt me.

I'm not sure why. My ears are like velvet, my paws smell like corn chips, and I have a superior sniffing nose.

I'm a catch.

So I was packed up and sent to an adoption event in Toronto, Canada, and that's where I met her—my forever owner, Meghan Markle.

I absolutely adored Meghan.

Meghan and I did everything together: we went on walks,

played fetch, even binge-watched episodes of *Suits*.

But I wasn't the only one. A human loved Meghan too.

His name was Harry.

He was tall, debonair,
and had hair the color of
a traffic cone.
But more important,
he was a prince—
the kind you read about
in fairy tales
and supermarket tabloids.

Prince Harry loved Meghan so much
he asked her to marry him.

Which meant Meghan was going to be a ~~princess~~ duchess,

and I was going to be a ROYAL DOG!

I was so excited that I chased my tail for twenty-four hours straight.

But I was
also nervous.

After all, I didn't have
fancy pedigree papers.
I was just a regular dog
who put his collar on
one neck at a time.
I wasn't sure if
I would fit in.

I knew Meghan had to get the queen's consent
to marry Harry. But would she welcome
me to the royal family too?
Meghan scratched my head and said, "Don't worry, Guy.
The royal family loves dogs—especially Queen Elizabeth.
They'll fall in love with you and
your velvety ears and corn
chip paws just like I did."
It made me feel better.

So off to England we went, to go start our new lives at Kensington Palace.

And what a palace it was!

There were huge fireplaces to curl up next to,
antique furniture legs to gnaw on . . .

. . . and the royal guards were all wearing black poodles on their head for some reason.

The palace gardens were incredible too.
There were so many proper and
well-mannered squirrels.

It was dog *heaven!*

But my transition to English life wasn't all kibble and roses.

I was confused by their customs.

In England, dogs go to the bathroom on the left side of the hydrant.

Instead of sneakers, they chew on *trainers*.

And my doggie sweater was replaced

with something called a doggie *jumper*.

Things got bad when I met
Queen Elizabeth's royal canines:
Sir Vulcan the Great, and
Madame Candy the Equally Great.

"Hello," I said.

"Pip-pip cheerio collywobbles
Bob's your uncle," replied Vulcan.

"Pardon me," I said. "I don't speak British."

"Very well," said Vulcan. "As a royal dog, you never say an uncouth 'hello' when greeting someone. You bow with your neck, like this."

"Oh, I'm sorry," I said.

"No. No. No," said Candy.

"You never say 'I'm sorry,' either.

You blame it on the prime minister.

Such as, 'The prime minister is the one

who made that mess on the carpet.'"

I was embarrassed.

I had so much to learn about being a royal dog.

Meanwhile, Meghan and Harry were busy getting ready for the wedding.
There were gowns to try on, cakes to taste, flowers to arrange, and
handwritten wedding invitations to send out to all 65 million Britons.

They inspired me.
I was determined to be
the perfect royal dog for them.

So I enrolled in the prestigious Westminster Doggy Obedience Academy, which boasts such illustrious graduates as:

WINSTON BARKHILL

"We shall chase tennis balls on the beaches; we shall chase tennis balls in the fields and in the streets; we shall never surrender chasing tennis balls."

CHARLES DOGWIN

Writer of the groundbreaking text
The Origin of Belly Rubs

RINGO STARR

Beatle

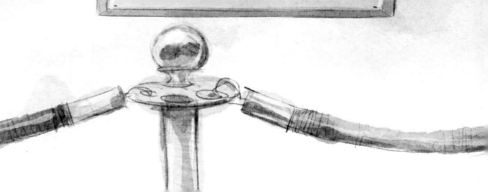

But despite all my training, I kept messing up.

I shed hair
on the throne.

I ate half of Prince Charles's
Cornish Yarg sandwich.

I dragged my butt on
the palace carpets.

I ate the other half of
Prince Charles's
Cornish Yarg
sandwich.

Things got so bad that Vulcan pulled me aside and said,
"Tallyho, you're off your trolley, you cheeky chuckaboo."

Which roughly translates to,
"You'll never get the queen's consent
to be a royal dog acting like that."

. . . were equally unkind.

The Doggy Mail

200 YEAR OLD MIRACLE DEWORMING FORMULA FOUND!

FAUX PAW!
GUY TRACKS MUD ON ROYAL CARPET

BIGFOOT HAS A PET PUG

I felt like I was back in the woods of Kentucky: lost and alone.

And then the big day came: the royal wedding!

It was incredible! The pageantry, the crowds, the ridiculous hats!

Meghan looked gorgeous! Harry looked handsome!

Everything was absolutely perfect.

Everything except for one thing: me.

Who was I fooling? I wasn't a royal dog.

I was going to ruin Meghan and Harry's special day.

I was feeling hopeless when in walked
Queen Elizabeth. She looked upset,
and I thought for sure it was
because of me.

But to my surprise, the queen said,
"Oh dear, Guy, I can't find the sprig
of myrtle for Meghan's bouquet.
It's been a part of every royal bouquet
since the 1840s. I simply must
find another one."

I knew what I had to do. I ran out the doggie door, put my superior beagle nose to the ground, and searched the palace gardens for the myrtle plant—a scent I knew all too well from my days in the Kentucky woods.

I sniffed on top of statues. I sniffed in the fountain. I sniffed around hedges.

I sniffed everywhere until—*brilliant!*—I found it! I grabbed a small sprig in my teeth and ran back to the queen as fast as my legs would carry me, feeling rightly chuffed. (Hey! I was getting the hang of this British thing after all.)

The queen was overjoyed.

Even Vulcan and Candy were impressed, shouting, "Scrummy hunky-dory!" Which translates to "Who's a good boy?"

Seizing the moment, I climbed up in the queen's lap and asked,
"Your Majesty, now may I please be a royal dog?"

The queen just laughed and said, "My dear Guy.
You don't have to save the day to be a royal dog.
And it doesn't matter if you're a purebred corgi
from Wales or stray dog from Kentucky.
All that matters is that after the
wedding, we will be a family."

"Really?"
I said, moved.

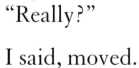

"Yes," said the queen. "You don't have to be something you're not, you only have to be what you are. And what you are is a smart little beagle with velvety ears who is loved by Meghan and Harry and now me."

I smiled and licked the queen's face.

I was about to become a royal dog!

With that, the queen leapt to her feet—well, slowly got up; she is ninety-two years old—and said, "Let's go for a ride, Guy. We have to get this bouquet to Meghan."

"Can we both stick our heads out the window?" I asked.

"Absolutely," said the queen.

And that's exactly what we did,
all the way to the royal wedding.

THE END

Simon & Schuster
1230 Avenue of the Americas
New York, NY 10020

First Simon & Schuster hardcover edition November 2018

SIMON & SCHUSTER and colophon are registered trademarks of Simon & Schuster, Inc.

For information about special discounts for bulk purchases,
please contact Simon & Schuster Special Sales at 1-866-506-1949 or business@simonandschuster.com.

The Simon & Schuster Speakers Bureau can bring authors to your live event.
For more information or to book an event contact the
Simon & Schuster Speakers Bureau at 1-866-248-3049 or visit our website at www.simonspeakers.com.

Interior design by Ruth Lee-Mui

Manufactured in the United States of America

1   3   5   7   9   10   8   6   4   2

Library of Congress Cataloging-in-Publication Data has been applied for.

ISBN 978-1-9821-1462-6
ISBN 978-1-9821-1463-3 (ebook)